a dOG's BReak Bfast!

CONTENTS

FOREWORD 4
INTRODUCTION 8
THE MORE THINGS CHANGE ...
THE MORE THEY STAY THE SAME 10
2020, A DOG'S BREAKFAST! 14
POLITICAL CARTOONIST OF THE YEAR 16
ALL OVER THE PLACE 26
BURIED BONES 40
WHAT THE PUP!?! 52
STUCK IN THE KENNEL 68
DOG-EAT-DOG 84
OFF THE LEASH 98
NOT LETTING SLEEPING DOGS LIE 114
ABOUT THE ARTISTS 130

FOREWORD: MY BRIEF LIFE WITH CARTOONS

Peter C Doherty
Laureate Professor
Patron of the Doherty Institute

It was kind of a buzz when I was invited earlier this year to be a judge of the year's best political cartoonist.

After following my standard protocol of making sure it didn't involve any real effort (I am an Australian male), I accepted with alacrity. And it was an intriguing experience. People of my generation are accustomed to seeing cartoonists strut their stuff, day in day out, in one or other newspaper, but we don't normally look at their collected works.

We went through the judging process at home alone and then, in the spirit of 2020, the small judging panel had an amiable Zoom meeting, where everyone agreed that all the cartoonists were terrific, but that one particular person seemed to have covered all the bases superbly well and so was our unanimous pick. As the very definite outsider with absolutely no expertise in the visual arts, I found it gratifying to find that I was on the same page as those who actually knew what they were doing.

Thinking about it later, I recalled a distant time when, very briefly, I was cartoon-worthy. Digging through the 'dusty' (albeit digital) archive, I found cartoons signed by Warren Brown, Peter Nicholson and Cathy Wilcox. Back then, I had been selected as the 1997 Australian of the Year, a process that (unlike the practice today) involved a small committee sitting around in a Sydney office making a quick decision so that they could get on with knocking off a couple of bottles of supplied Grange (my impression, not based in evidence). The only problem was that my wife,

Penny, and I had been living in Memphis, Tennessee, for the past eight years. Nevertheless, we flew to Melbourne and turned up at the Sidney Myer Music Bowl on 26 January to receive the award from then Prime Minister John Howard.

Having been enormously busy with the Nobel Prize events and what followed, I'd taken no notice of what was happening in Australian politics. As a consequence, it hadn't occurred to me that it was a bit off the point to congratulate Howard on the progress Australia was making towards becoming a republic. One cartoon had me vaccinating John against the republic (he was already immune). Pointedly, Cathy Wilcox finished her cartoon (which lists a lot of issues we're still addressing now) with: 'And the Australian of the Year prefers to live overseas!'

Being a guest judge this year was illuminating, but it was a bit sad to get the sense that some cartoonists were pulling their punches on certain subjects — climate change, cancel culture — that a particular readership might not wish to confront.

We're now facing some very real and dangerous problems. Satirists, at least, should be able to address them. Scientists like me do their best to tell the truth and, so far as I'm concerned, that's what also characterises great journalists, great editors and great cartoonists. I've always had the sense that part of the job of the

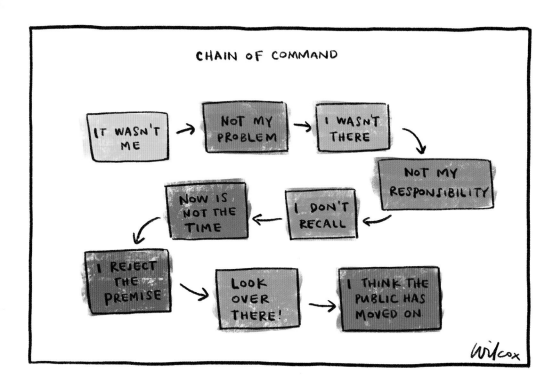

cartoonist in an open democracy is to provoke us, and maybe to make us a bit angry, so that we suddenly have doubts about some entrenched position, some dogmatic idea of how things are, or should be.

Peter C Doherty
September 2020

Laureate Professor Peter Doherty is Patron of the Doherty Institute, Melbourne. He was awarded the Nobel Prize in Physiology or Medicine in 1996, and named Australian of the Year in 1997. He was a guest judge for *Behind the Lines 2020*.

INTRODUCTION

Daryl Karp
Director
Museum of Australian Democracy

It has been a year of disruption, but also of magnificent resilience. Nothing about 2020 has been 'business as usual': the Museum of Australian Democracy has navigated unexpected closures due to bushfires, hailstorms and the pandemic.

However, thanks to the efforts of our exemplary team of professionals, we have managed to bring this 'dog' of a year to heel and close it out with the launch of yet another outstanding *Behind the Lines* exhibition. We recognise that now, perhaps more than ever, many of our visitors deeply appreciate their annual pilgrimage to our most popular and enduring exhibition.

We have added a few new elements in the latest edition. For the first time we are presenting a selection of cartoons in digital form. The use of pertinent drawings animated into gifs reflects some of the innovative ways our cartoonists are now working. Our new onsite 'In Focus' section will closely examine an issue of particular significance and how it has been considered through the last decade or so of cartooning. For this first iteration we are delighted that journalist Amy McQuire is helping to unpack the annual Closing the Gap reports and how cartoonists have responded since 2007. The panel deciding our Political Cartoonist of the Year was expanded. This year, it was graced by guest judges Laureate Professor Peter Doherty, Associate Professor Richard Scully, Marcus Hughes (the National Library of Australia's Director of Indigenous Engagement) and our guest curator Holly Williams, who complemented judges from the Museum (myself and Nanette Louchart-Fletcher took up the challenge this time around). The panel's collective eyes settled on Cathy Wilcox. This is the second time Cathy has been named as our Political Cartoonist of the Year; once again, we were struck by her unique voice and by the way she is able to capture the momentous events of the year as seen through the eyes of ordinary people. At a time when there seems to be a rapidly shrinking pool of female cartoonists, her cartoons present an appealing sense of whimsy and much-needed gentle humanity.

The tumultuous events of the year have provoked comparisons to the first half of the twentieth century and the global disruption and discord that characterised that period. As embattled journalists around the world constantly tell us, without a free press there can be no democracy. Never has a free and accurate media seemed more important. Despite the multifaceted challenges faced by traditional media platforms, we are still fortunate in this country to have a healthy and trusted media to turn to when times are tough. The cartoonists in this year's exhibition come from across the political spectrum. Yet each of them has brought their own robust interrogation of the goings-on in Canberra and of the seemingly endless cycle of press conferences. We are very lucky this year that they also found time to throw some light on some of our human foibles — a humble roll of toilet paper, for example, won't look quite the same after *Behind the Lines 2020*.

THE MORE THINGS CHANGE ... THE MORE THEY STAŸ THE SAME

Richard Scully
Associate Professor of Modern History
University of New England

In amongst all the dog-whistling, it's hard to think of another moment when so many disasters have converged on Australia (and the world) at once, and when these have affected people so personally, and to such an enormous extent.

Looking back through Australia's rich cartoon history, the obvious parallel is with the 'Spanish' 'flu pandemic of 1918–20, but perhaps we needn't cast our glance back quite that far to find a precedent for the other big themes of today. The Museum of Australian Democracy's archives offer us a place to start.

After the year we've had, we're pretty familiar with the anxieties and doomsaying that Will Mahony imagined in the *Daily News* on 28 January 1939 (see page 83). Cathy Wilcox's *Today's Anxiety Level* evokes his turn of phrase (see page 82). A lone prophet calls down from 'Mount Somewhere-or-Other', wailing about the end of everything (including 'impending frightfulness'). This was at a time when Parliament was closed for the summer recess, but Prime Minister Joe Lyons was worrying everyone about everything (if things were so bad, retorted Opposition Leader John Curtin, then why not reopen Parliament). And doomsayers were pointing to the deteriorating situation in Europe and Asia as rising great powers were rattling the sabre, and stoking the flames of hatred and war.

It would seem that the more things change, the more they stay the same. In 1968 it was Martin Luther King; in 2020 it's Ruth Bader Ginsburg. Today, the worlds of MLK and RBG don't seem so very far away from each other. John Frith's Melbourne *Herald* cartoon of 8 April 1968 (see p. 119) appeared just days after the great civil rights leader was gunned down in Memphis, at a time when more and more Americans were spilling out into the streets to vent their anger at an administration happy to stomp over moral standards and decency. President Lyndon Baines Johnson might have been a big bully, but at least he did have a moral compass and some intellect to speak of (unlike President Donald J Trump). And at least LBJ did champion aspects of civil rights at home even while he was trampling all over them in Asia. But, as usual, it would seem that DJT has gone one better (or worse) than his Democrat predecessor, as David Rowe suggests in *Bible Basher* (see page 118).

ScoMo's National Cabinet seems far less revolutionary when compared with the 'Premier's Plan' of the Great Depression era. Syd Miller's menagerie of state and federal leaders (*Smith's Weekly*, 13 June 1931) lacks social distancing, but suits our own latter-day economic crisis. And the huge political divisions within that group make today's rogues gallery seem relatively homogenous: Prime Minister Jim Scullin and Victorian and South Australian premiers Ned Hogan and Lionel Hill might have been Labor, and Western Australia's James Mitchell, Tassie's John McPhee and Queensland's Arthur Moore were basically just Nationalist/'Country Progressive' ancestors of today's Liberal-National Coalition. However, New South Wales' Jack Lang was probably as close to a socialist as we've come. He certainly

Syd Miller
Young Australia
Smith's Weekly, 13 June 1931

puts 'Chairman Dan' Andrews into perspective (and it's bizarre how much he looks like Freddie Mercury to modern eyes). And in amongst them are recognisable financial types — Sir Robert Gibson (Chairman of the Commonwealth Bank) and Sir Otto Niemeyer (an 'outside consultant' to the government) — who aren't far removed from today's experts, urging the 'tough decisions' to sustain the economy.

We might need to be reminded of the similarities between past and present, but it's worth remembering that at least one great cartoonist — and historian of cartoons — has lived through every one of these 'interesting' moments in time: Vane Lindesay, who celebrated his centenary on 2 October. As he would be able to tell you, even when history repeats itself — or, at least, rhymes — Australian cartoonists are never stuck for an idea, and are always just as innovative as ever they were.

Richard Scully
September 2020

Richard Scully is Associate Professor of Modern History at the University of New England. He is the author of *Eminent Victorian Cartoonists* (2018). He was a guest judge for *Behind the Lines 2020*.

2020
A DOG'S BREAKFAST!

In a year that some have politely described as 'a dog's breakfast', our theme encompasses 2020's mix of disruption and uncertainty. The term seems particularly fitting for something so unappealing — a year filled with mess, turmoil and failed attempts.

From the bushfire summer to the pandemic and global economic woes, Australia's political cartoonists have had plenty to work with. They have cast their eyes over the whole dog and pony show. There's the usual dog-eat-dog world of politics, with its top dogs, sly dogs and people thrown to the dogs. But they've also watched on as we've embraced panic buying, curves (on graphs and on ourselves) and experts in our midst (or at least at our press conferences). And masks. It's been a year with plenty of masks.

In this year's exhibition, visual cues from overlapping crises pepper the cartoons: Hawaiian shirts and burnt trees give way to masks and spiky balls. Fortunately, our cartoonists have also captured moments of goodness and humour amid the rolling drama. With luck, we can look back on 2020 — a masked, sloppy mess of a year — and send it firmly back to the doghouse where it belongs.

POLITICAL CARTOONIST OF THE YEAR

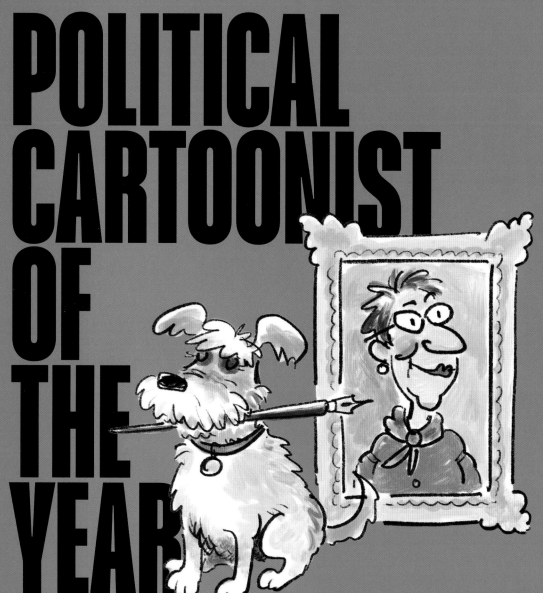

Through simple loose lines and splashes of colour Cathy Wilcox cuts egos down to size and draws out the best in us. This year she has pricked people's hearts with her take on events big and small. Reflecting on our nation, she has found a poignant angle to the summer's wildlife disaster and COVID-centric humour with 'any excuse to leave the house'.

Yet it is the sharp eye that she casts across both sides of politics that has made her such a deserving recipient of our Political Cartoonist of the Year award. This is the second time that Wilcox, a Sydney-based cartoonist for *The Sydney Morning Herald* and the Melbourne *Age*, has been named Political Cartoonist of the Year.

The warning signs have been there for years, but somehow, we've only just beginning to grasp the magnitude of the loss. These species, once common, are in danger of becoming extinct:

INTEGRITY

SHAME

HUMILITY

MORAL COURAGE

DECENCY

Meanwhile, these feral pests proliferate, while we stand by.

OPPORTUNISM

SELF-INTEREST

DECEIT

Wilcox

Cathy Wilcox
Endangered Species
The Sydney Morning Herald/The Age, 22 January 2020

Cathy Wilcox
Pray for Distraction

The Sydney Morning Herald/The Age, 28 January 2020

Cathy Wilcox
Bridge to Recovery
The Sydney Morning Herald/The Age, 7 October 2020

Cathy Wilcox
The Scorpion and the Frog
The Sydney Morning Herald/The Age, 28 May 2020

Cathy Wilcox
The New Casual

The Sydney Morning Herald, 29 July 2020

Cathy Wilcox
Lockdown Protest
The Sydney Morning Herald/The Age, 12 May 2020

Cathy Wilcox
Nostalgia
The Sydney Morning Herald/The Age, 11 August 2020

ALL OVER THE PLACE

RFS
RFS
RFS
RFS
RFS

After Australia's hottest and driest year on record in 2019, the summer's bushfires were unprecedented — everyone said so, ad nauseum. Some days it seemed the whole country was ablaze. During the crisis, our parliamentarians seemed to be all over the place too — one emergency services minister went to Europe and the prime minister jetted off on a Hawaiian holiday. Questions of leadership and preparation were thrashed out in the media. The role of climate change came to the fore as debate raged over the cause of the fires.

Matt Golding
The New Norm
The Sydney Morning Herald/The Age, 16 January 2020

Greg 'Smithy' Smith
A Sunburnt Country
Sunday Times (Perth), 5 January 2020

Bill Bramhall
So Much for New Year's Resolution to Quit Smoking
New York Daily News, 1 February 2020

Greg 'Smithy' Smith
Uses for Another Bushfire Enquiry

In a newspaper conference room...

Mark David
Climate Awareness
Independent Australia, 12 January 2020

Peter Broelman
Flattening, Flattering
Syndicated, 14 April 2020

David Rowe
Thoughts and Prayers
The Australian Financial Review, 11 November 2019

Glen Le Lievre
Flat Out

Patreon, 18 December 2019

Sean Leahy
Fuel for the Firestorm
The Courier-Mail, 4 January 2020

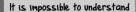
It is impossible to understand

Even though these unprecedented fires are beyond enormous, some creatures manage to survive them. Then when the fire has passed they begin to starve.

When (if) the rains do come it is too late, they simply starve to death in the mud.

More than a billion creatures died – are still dying – in just nsw and victoria alone – almost 80 species have had more than a third of their habitat erased – the huge biomass of the countless insects smashed to pieces.

Some of it will return as it was – much of it will not. Whatever happens it is transformed forever as the climate is transformed forever.

We see the sad and hopeful stories – this koala escaping the flames, a kangaroo fleeing through the smoke, the scorched dam surrounded by thirsty lyrebirds a possum clinging to a firey's helmet.

MIRACLE KOALA

SURVIVES FIRES*

 * DIES LATER

And then of course the hail came and killed so many more.... on it goes on it goes

A huge rescue effort is underway some people are as lovely as other people are terrible. They are dropping sweet potatoes from helicopters.

There is a vast crew of vets and nurses and thousands of volunteers helping heal and feed and soothe and rehabilitate and letting go those who can't be healed. The survivors can't always be returned home as their homes are gone.

When we see ourselves through the prism of custodianship of the land and its' creatures we are at our best.

At our worst we fill our parliaments with smirking grifters and surrender to the siren song of greed that tells us we are powerless to escape our doom.

There is always hope, it is battered and burnt around the edges and sometimes goes missing altogether – but there it is again. It is a volunteer getting up night after night to bottle feed an orphan joey every three hours – a stranger saving a koala from the flames in her shirt, they even have koala rescue dogs now!

Hope is unfortunately other people, and we are all we have.

First Dog on the Moon
Saving the Animals
37   *Guardian Australia*, 29 January 2020

Matt Golding
Our Plan
The Sydney Morning Herald/The Age, 20 December 2019

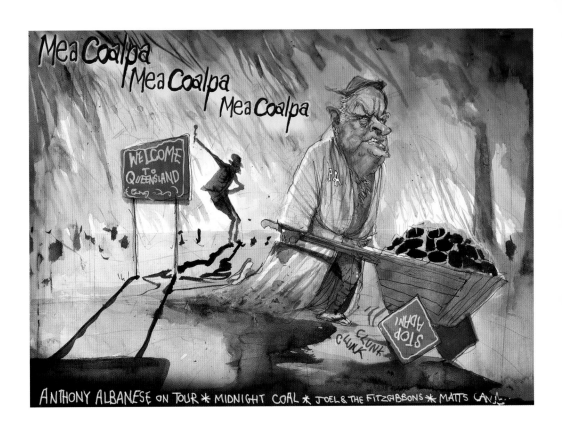

David Rowe
Mea Coalpa
The Australian Financial Review, 10 December 2019

BURIED BONES

Scoops, scandals and secrets are the juicy bones that newshounds sniff out and dig up. They provide much-needed distractions from the momentous events unfolding across the nation and the globe. 2020 offered up the old favourites of party infighting, branch-stacking and alleged pork-barrelling. Headline writers got a gift with a scandal that rhymed: 'sports rorts'.

Meanwhile, buried bones of a different sort prompted the Department of Home Affairs to consider domestic surveillance. And the 'robodebt' debacle refused to go away quietly.

Lindsay Foyle
The Virus
New Matilda, 6 August 2020

Matt Golding
Owing Something to Someone
The Sydney Morning Herald/The Age, 2 June 2020

Jon Kudelka
Roast Pork
The Saturday Paper, 25 January 2020

Matt Golding
Herding Nats

The Sydney Morning Herald/The Age, 19 February 2020

Simon Kneebone
Australians' Access to Information — Redacted
Australian Socialist, 1 March 2020

Mark Knight
Feeling Irrelevant

Herald Sun, 20 June 2020

Fiona Katauskas
Hitting the (Far) Right Note
Eureka Street, 5 May 2020

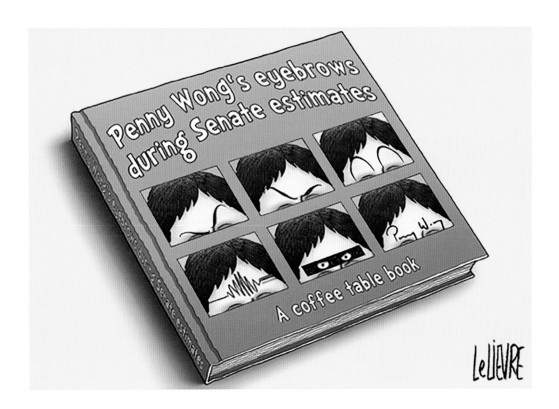

Glen Le Lievre
The Eyes Have It
The Australian, 9 March 2020

Michael Leunig
Political Pandemic
The Sydney Morning Herald/The Age, 6 July 2020

David Pope
A Measure of Trust
The Canberra Times, 23 April 2020

WHAT THE PUP!?!

An almost invisible agent created the upheaval of the century. Its impact was so swift and widespread it left many people's heads spinning.

Our cartoonists charted the arrival of the coronavirus, at first from a distance and then from very, very close to home. They offered up visuals (and a gag or two) to help us make sense of our shock and our fears. And they worked hard to illuminate the heaviness of closed borders and lockdowns. From Melbourne, cartoonists caught in Victoria's second wave shone a light on the inequality and economic fears and the ever-present face of Premier Daniel Andrews.

Judy Horacek
Upside-down World
Now or Never, Horacek Press, 2019

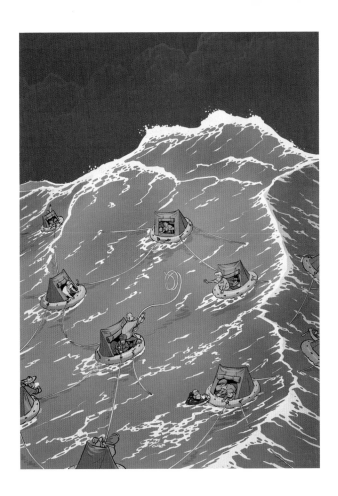

David Pope
Holding Together, Keeping Apart

The Canberra Times, 14 April 2020

Christopher Downes
Going Out Like a Lamb ...
The Mercury, 31 March 2020

Matt Golding
Stopping the Australian Spread
The Sydney Morning Herald/The Age, 2 April 2020

Peter Broelman
Parliament Dropout

Syndicated, 16 April 2020

Johannes Leak
Untitled
The Australian, 10 August 2020

Jon Kudelka
Little Red Bottom Line

THE HIDDEN BENEFITS OF A REMOTE SENATE

Christopher Downes
The Hidden Benefits of a Remote Senate
The Mercury, 25 August 2020

David Rowe
COVID City Circle

The Australian Financial Review, 4 August 2020

Dean Alston
Here's Your Ball Back
The West Australian, 8 July 2020

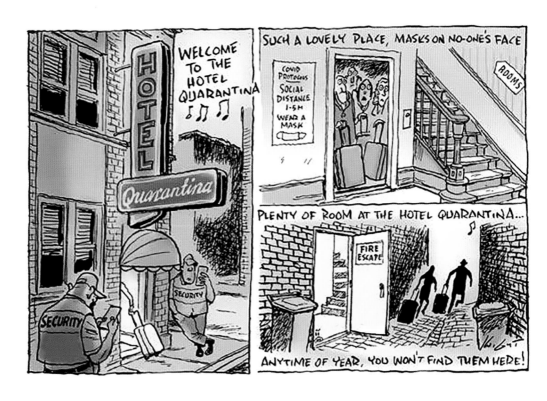

Mark Knight
Hotel Quarantina
Herald Sun, 18 August 2020

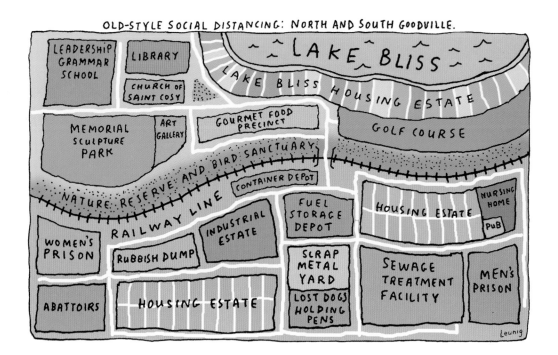

Michael Leunig
Social Distancing Goodville
The Sydney Morning Herald/The Age, 2 May 2020

Glen Le Lievre
Middle Dan

Patreon, 30 June 2020

STUCK IN THE KENNEL

When news came in that millions of people, first in China and then in Italy, had been placed in strict virus quarantine, few in Australia thought that would happen here. Infection numbers rising and spreading around the globe gave us an inkling of what lay ahead. 'The Pando' had arrived.

The nation seemed to respond as one — rushing out to clear store shelves of toilet paper. Home became the new office, school and gym. Hope and fear went head to head. We went 'doom scrolling' and added new words like 'iso' and 'sanny' to our daily lives.

John Shakespeare
End Times
The Sydney Morning Herald/The Age, 5 March 2020

Andrew Dyson
The Apocalypse Handicap

The Sydney Morning Herald/The Age, 4 March 2020

Matt Golding
The Second Wave of Hoarding
The Sydney Morning Herald/The Age, 23 June 2020

Glen Le Lievre
TP Fort

Patreon, 30 June 2020

Johannes Leak
Untitled
The Australian, 3 April 2020

Andrew Weldon
Some Expressions to Avoid
The Big Issue, 15 March 2020

John Ditchburn
I Call It Poetic Justice
The Courier (Ballarat), 31 July 2020

Fiona Katauskas
Wrongs and Rights
Eureka Street, 28 July 2020

Chris 'Roy' Taylor
Life in Lockdown
Self-published, 16 April 2020

WORKING FROM HOME

Glen Le Lievre
Working from Home

Patreon, 3 March 2020

Michael Leunig
Flattening the Curve
The Sydney Morning Herald/The Age, 6 April 2020

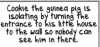

First Dog on the Moon
Pets of the Pandemic
Guardian Australia, 30 March 2020

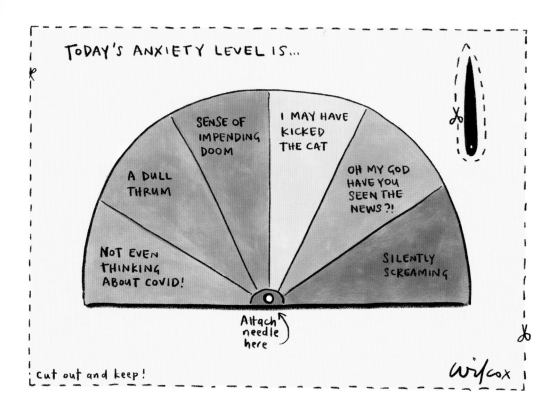

Cathy Wilcox
Today's Anxiety Level
The Sydney Morning Herald/The Age, 5 August 2020

DOG-
EAT-
DOG

Leading in a crisis can be like walking a tightrope. Put a foot wrong, and you risk losing the nation's trust or worse. When people's lives are turned upside-down, a spark can set off widespread unrest.

The pandemic has shown us an international kaleidoscope of leadership styles. Some have fostered strong community bonds and a 'team spirit', while others have used it to promote discord and capitalise on the disruption for their own ends. Parliaments around the world have been forced to do things differently, often stress-testing the resilience of institutions and agreements.

David Rowe
Snookered
The Australian Financial Review, 28 March 2020

THE EASTER RESURRECTION

Eric Löbbecke
Ride 'Em, Vladimir
The Australian, 9 May 2020

David Pope
Not Helping

The Canberra Times, 4 June 2020

Jim Pavlidis
Watchful
The Sydney Morning Herald/The Age, 31 March 2020

Eric Löbbecke
One for the Belt and Road
The Australian, 30 April 2020

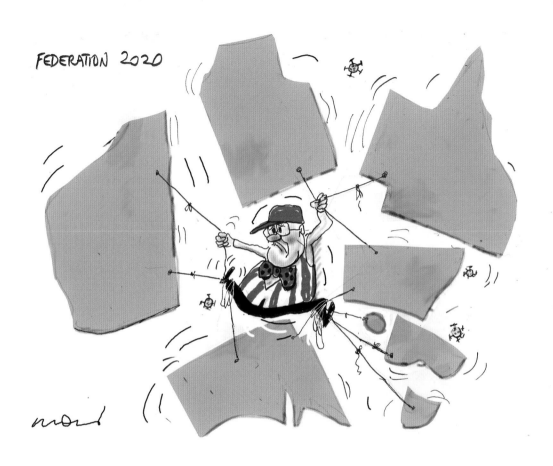

Alan Moir
Federation

Self-published, 17 August 2020

Brett Lethbridge
Open and Shut Case
The Courier-Mail, 6 August 2020

Dean Alston
Iron Mark
95   *The West Australian*, 6 April 2020

Cathy Wilcox
Hasta la Vista
The Sydney Morning Herald/The Age, 19 August 2020

Cathy Wilcox
The What?
97   *The Sydney Morning Herald*, 17 September 2020

OFF THE LEASH

2020 was going to be so good.
The economy was going to be
'back in black', and we were
going to bring home gold from
the Tokyo Olympic Games.
But the Games were nixed, and
the economic tide turned. By
September Australia had entered
its first recession in almost three
decades. Globally, the picture
was even worse.

Here, eye-wateringly large
stimulus packages were
rolled out by state and federal
governments. Our cartoonists
were kept busy as industries were
dubbed 'winners' or 'losers' in
the cash splash.

Warren Brown
Recession
Daily Telegraph, 4 June 2020

Jon Kudelka
Having Your Cake
The Saturday Paper, 14 May 2020

John Shakespeare
The Ghost of Kevin
The Sydney Morning Herald/The Age, 1 April 2020

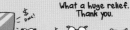
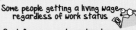
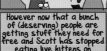

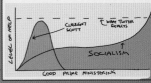

Alan Moir
We're All in This Together
The Sydney Morning Herald/The Age, 16 May 2020

Fiona Katauskas
Cancelling Culture
Eureka Street, 11 August 2020

Christopher Downes
Talking Back the Support
The Mercury, 9 June 2020

John Shakespeare
How Good Was Holden?
The Sydney Morning Herald/The Age, 23 February 2020

Jon Kudelka
The Long-range Forecast
The Saturday Paper, 4 June 2020

Mark Knight
The Odd Couple
Herald Sun, 27 May 2020

John Spooner
Snap Back Economics
The Australian, 19 May 2020

Mark Knight
Almost Got This Thing Flattened
Herald Sun, 7 September 2020

Cathy Wilcox
Mastermind
The Sydney Morning Herald, 4 September 2020

Fiona Katauskas
Going with the Flow
Eureka Street, 7 October 2020

NOT LETTING SLEEPING DOGS LIE

COVID-19's radical disruption of the status quo brought various underlying systemic problems to the fore. The American Black Lives Matter movement triggered protests in many countries. But it was the rising number of First Nations people dying in custody that lay at the heart of the protests in Australia. Other protests challenged inaction on climate change, a multinational company's destructive act, coronavirus lockdowns — and even the rollout of a wireless technology.

With free speech front and centre, cartoonists also turned their attention to the role of social media, privacy and public interest journalism.

Danny Eastwood
Untitled
The Koori Mail, 1 July 2020

Danny Eastwood
Untitled
117 *The Koori Mail*, 17 June 2020

David Rowe
Bible Basher
The Financial Review, 5 June 2020

John Frith
Untitled
The Herald, 8 April 1968

Johannes Leak
Untitled
The Australian, 12 June 2020

Christopher Downes
Anti-social Distancing
The Mercury, 20 July 2020

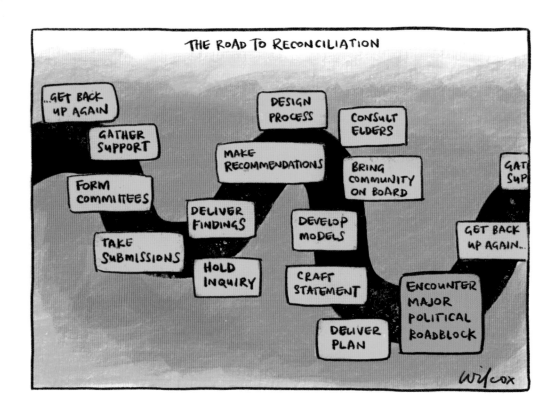

Cathy Wilcox
Road to Reconciliation
The Sydney Morning Herald/The Age, 27 May 2020

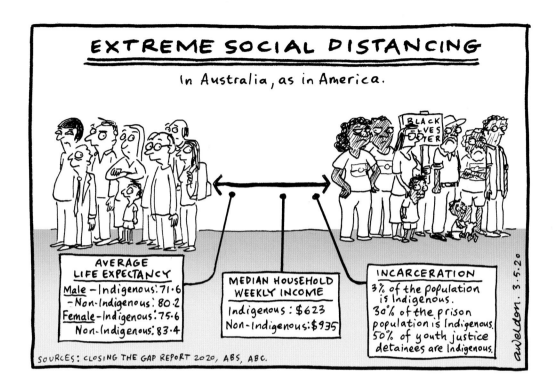

Andrew Weldon
Extreme Social Distancing
The Big Issue, 3 May 2020

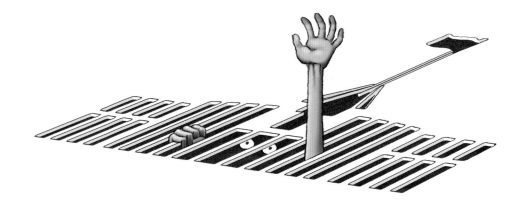

Glen Le Lievre
Not Drowning
Patreon, 4 December 2019

David Pope
Rio Tinto Blows It
The Canberra Times, 28 May 2020

Matt Golding
A Historical Perspective
The Sydney Morning Herald/The Age, 11 June 2020

Jon Kudelka
The Underpants of Democracy

Mark Knight
Privacy Concerns
Herald Sun, 20 April 2020

John Spooner
Greed
The Australian, 24 April 2020

ABOUT THE ARTISTS

Dean Alston

Dean Alston is an editorial cartoonist for *The West Australian*. A past Walkley Award–winner for best cartoon, Alston has also worked as a cartographer and publican.

Bill Bramhall

Bill Bramhall is an American illustrator and is the editorial cartoonist for the *New York Post*.

Peter Broelman

Peter Broelman is a nationally syndicated editorial cartoonist based in Adelaide. He has won three Stanley Awards for his editorial cartoons and, in 2005 and 2009, was awarded the prestigious Gold Stanley for Cartoonist of the Year. His work appears in regional newspapers, including *The Geelong Advertiser* and the *Sunshine Coast Daily*, and on his website.

Warren Brown

Warren Brown is the editorial cartoonist for *The Daily Telegraph* (Sydney), for which he also writes a weekly motoring column. Brown has won three Stanley Awards for best editorial cartoon.

Mark David

Mark David is a Queensland-based cartoonist who has previously worked for *The Australian Financial Review*, *The Bulletin*, *The Sydney Morning Herald* and several other publications around the world. He currently produces political cartoons for the online news journal *Independent Australia*.

John Ditchburn

John Ditchburn has been the cartoonist for *The Courier* (Ballarat) since 1990. He is also regularly published in *The Farmer*. His work has featured in numerous international educational books. He won the Quill Award for Best Cartoon in 2006 and 2013, and has been shortlisted six times.

Christopher Downes

Christopher Downes draws two cartoons a week for the Hobart *Mercury*. He has also drawn many works for the Museum of Australian Democracy, Canberra and the *Lore* podcast. He also works at Museum of Old and New Art, Hobart, where his mind is being slowly corrupted.

Andrew Dyson

Andrew Dyson is a dual Walkley Award–winning cartoonist and illustrator for *The Age* in Melbourne.

Danny Eastwood

Danny Eastwood is a member of the Ngemba Tribe of western New South Wales. For more than two decades, Eastwood has made his living as an artist doing commercial work, including cartoons, for the *Koori Mail* and for companies such as Coca-Cola. He has also created various pieces of public art and murals around Sydney. He has won numerous awards for his artwork, including NAIDOC Artist of the Year, the NAIDOC Poster Competition and the Parliament of New South Wales Aboriginal Art Prize.

First Dog on the Moon

'First Dog on the Moon' is the pseudonym for Andrew Marlton, the Walkley Award-winning political cartoonist for *Guardian Australia*. He has written and illustrated various books, illustrated numerous others, performed live on stage in a number of shows and is currently working on 'more exciting projects than you can poke a stick at', including another book. He was the MoAD Political Cartoonist of the Year in 2011.

Lindsay Foyle

Lindsay Foyle has been drawing cartoons professionally since 1975. His work has appeared in *The Bulletin* and *The Australian*. He is a past president of the Australian Cartoonists' Association.

Glen Le Lievre
Toast
Patreon, 20 December 2019

John Frith

John Frith (1906–2000) was one of Australia's most prominent and prolific cartoonists for more than four decades years. His work was printed in *The Bulletin*, *The Sydney Morning Herald* and Melbourne's *Herald* over his long career. He was also a sculptor and potter, and many of his cartoons and ceramic works are held in the Museum of Australian Democracy's collection.

Matt Golding

Matt Golding is a political cartoonist with the Melbourne *Age* and Sunday *Age*. He draws weekly cartoons for the *Melbourne Times*, *The Melbourne Weekly Magazine* and *The Sunday Age*. He also contributes to *The Sydney Morning Herald* and a range of other publications and corporate clients. He has won a Walkley Award and seven Stanley Awards. He was MoAD Political Cartoonist of the Year in 2018.

Judy Horacek

Judy Horacek is a freelance cartoonist and picture book creator. Her cartoons have been published widely in newspapers and magazines, including *The Australian*, *The Canberra Times* and *The Sydney Morning Herald*. They currently appear regularly in the *Melbourne Age*. She has published nine collections of her cartoons.

Fiona Katauskas

Fiona Katauskas is a freelance cartoonist based in Sydney. Her political work has been published in a wide range of newspapers and magazines, including the *Melbourne Age*, *The Australian*, *The Sydney Morning Herald* and *The Bulletin*, and currently appears regularly in *Eureka Street*.

Simon Kneebone

Simon Kneebone is an Adelaide-based freelance cartoonist and illustrator. His work has appeared in the *New Internationalist*, the website *Pro Bono*, and the journal *Australian Options*.

Mark Knight

Mark Knight is an editorial cartoonist for the Melbourne *Herald Sun* and *Sunday Herald Sun*. Knight previously worked for the *Australian Financial Review* and the *Melbourne Herald*. He won the Gold Quill Award in 2005 for the best cartoon of the year and has also won several Walkley Awards. He was MoAD's Political Cartoonist of the Year in 2014.

Jon Kudelka

Jon Kudelka is a freelance cartoonist based in Hobart. His work appears in the Hobart *Mercury*, *The Saturday Paper* and on his website. Until recently his work also appeared in *The Australian*, but he has moved on to spend more time on his new gallery, The Kudelka Shop, in Salamanca Place, Hobart. In 2008 Kudelka won the Walkley Award for best cartoon and the Stanley Award for best political cartoonist. He won the Walkley again in 2018 and the Kennedy Award for best cartoon in 2019. He was MoAD's Political Cartoonist of the Year for 2019.

Sean Leahy

Sean Leahy is a political cartoonist for the Brisbane *Courier-Mail*. He also writes and draws the comic strip *Beyond the Black Stump*. He was previously cartoonist for Brisbane's *Sunday Mail*, *Sunday Sun* and *Daily Sun*, as well as Perth's *Sunday Times* and *The West Australian*. In 2000 Leahy was awarded a Churchill Fellowship to undertake research into cartooning overseas.

Johannes Leak

Johannes Leak is an illustrator based just north of Sydney. After formal art training at the Julian Ashton Art School, he explored figurative painting for some years before switching to both natural media and digital illustration. He has been working as a freelancer ever since, specialising in cartooning, caricature, storyboarding and commercial art. He contributes regularly to *The Australian* and *Tracks* surfing magazine. He is also the illustrator of Claire Garth's *Grover McBane, Rescue Dog* children's book series.

Brett Lethbridge

Brett Lethbridge is the editorial cartoonist for the Brisbane *Courier-Mail*. He has also been published in the *Sunday Mail* and *West Australian*.

Michael Leunig

Michael Leunig is an Australian cartoonist, writer, painter, philosopher and poet. His commentary on political, cultural and emotional life spans more than 50 years. He often explores the idea of an innocent and sacred personal world and the fragile ecosystem of human nature and its relationship to the wider natural world. His newspaper work appears regularly in *The Age* and *The Sydney Morning Herald*.

Glen Le Lievre

Glen Le Lievre's drawings have appeared in the *Melbourne Age*, *The Sydney Morning Herald*, *MAD*, *Private Eye*, *Reader's Digest*, *The New Yorker*, *Time* and the *Wall Street Journal*.

Eric Löbbecke

Eric Löbbecke is an award-winning illustrator and cartoonist for books, newspapers, magazines and advertising since 1988. He has worked for News Limited on *The Australian* and the Sydney *Sunday Telegraph* and *Daily Telegraph*. He has won Walkley and Stanley awards for illustration and two Bald Archy Prizes for satirical portraiture.

Will Mahony

Francis William 'Will' Mahony (1905–1989) was an Australian cartoonist and printmaker, most widely associated with Sydney's *Daily News*, *Daily Telegraph* and *Daily Mirror*.

Syd Miller

In a long career, Syd Miller (1901–1983) drew cartoons for many publications, including *The Bulletin*, *Smith's Weekly*, the Sydney *Sun*, the Melbourne *Herald* and the *Daily Telegraph*. In 1938 he helped devise the iconic 'Chesty Bond' figure for the Bond's clothing company, and in the 1950s created the 'A Little Bear Will Fix It' comic to advertise Behr-Manning's brand of adhesive tape.

Alan Moir

Alan Moir is an editorial cartoonist for *The Sydney Morning Herald*. He has also worked for *The Bulletin* and the Brisbane *Courier-Mail*. He has won three Stanley Awards, two Walkley Awards and the prestigious Gold Stanley Award.

Jim Pavlidis

Jim Pavlidis is an award-winning painter and illustrator. He has been at the Melbourne *Age* for 30 years. He won a Melbourne Press Club Quill Award for best artwork in 2015 and for best cartoon in 2019. His most recent publication, *Kitchen Sink Drama*, features his illustrations accompanying Paul Connolly's 100-word vignettes.

David Pope

David Pope worked as a freelance cartoonist and illustrator for many years, including at the Sydney *Sun-Herald*, before joining *The Canberra Times* as a staff artist in 2008 after the retirement of local cartooning legend Geoff Pryor. His cartoons have appeared in range of publications, including *AEU News*, *Arena*, *Common Cause*, *The Diplomat*, *Hard Hat*, *The New Doctor*, the *Northern Rivers Echo*, *Overland*, *The Queensland Nurse* and *The Republican*. He was MoAD's Political Cartoonist of the Year in 2012.

David Rowe

David Rowe is a daily editorial cartoonist for the *Australian Financial Review*. Rowe has won numerous awards for his political cartooning, including being named MoAD's Political Cartoonist of the Year in 2013 and 2017.

John Shakespeare

John Shakespeare is a Walkley Award–winning illustrator and cartoonist for *The Sydney Morning Herald*. He has previously worked for the Brisbane *Courier-Mail* and the *Sydney Sun*.

Greg 'Smithy' Smith

'Smithy' was born in Perth, Western Australia. He started his cartooning life at Perth's *Daily News* and is now editorial cartoonist for the Perth *Sunday Times* and *Seven West Media*.

John Spooner

John Spooner was cartoonist and editorial illustrator for *The Age*, where he worked for 42 years until his redundancy in 2016. As well as being widely published, Spooner has won five Stanley awards, four Walkley awards, the Graeme Perkin award in 2002 and the Fremantle Print Prize (shared) in 1986.

Chris 'Roy' Taylor

Chris 'Roy' Taylor has been a professional cartoonist and illustrator for over 25 years and his work also appears in the Melbourne *Herald Sun*. He creates daily cartoons and illustrations and, in 2014, also published a children's book, *The Great Big Book of Aussie Inventions*.

Andrew Weldon

Andrew Weldon is a freelance cartoonist whose work appears regularly in the Melbourne *Age* and *The Big Issue*. His work has also appeared in *Private Eye*, *The Spectator* and *The New Yorker*. Weldon has published several children's books, including the *Don't Look Now* series with Paul Jennings, as well as two collections of his cartoons.

Cathy Wilcox

Cathy Wilcox is a Sydney-based cartoonist for *The Sydney Morning Herald* and the Melbourne *Age*. She has published two collections of her cartoons, and has illustrated numerous children's books. Wilcox has won three Walkley Awards for cartooning and several Stanley Awards for single-gag and political cartoons. In 2016 she was MoAD's Political Cartoonist of the Year, as she is again in 2020.

Published 2020 by the Museum of Australian Democracy at Old Parliament House

PO Box 3934, Manuka ACT 2603
Phone: 02 6270 8222
Email: info@moadoph.gov.au
Website: moadoph.gov.au

ISBN: 978-0-646-82195-5
ISSN: 1835 3452

Exhibition curator: Holly Williams
Writer: Holly Williams
Researcher: Fiona Katauskas
Foreword: Peter Doherty
Introduction: Daryl Karp
Essay: Richard Scully
Front cover illustration: Cathy Wilcox
Designer: Studio Starr
Publisher's editor: Robert Nichols

Behind the Lines is a travelling exhibition developed by the Museum of Australian Democracy at Old Parliament House, proudly supported by the National Collecting Institutions Touring and Outreach Program.

An Australian Government program aiming to improve access to national collections for all Australians.

For more information about the *Behind the Lines* exhibition: moadoph.gov.au/BTL

Front cover:
Cathy Wilcox
2020, A Dog's Breakfast!
Behind the Lines
September 2020